Women
Are From
Venus

MEN
Are From
HELL

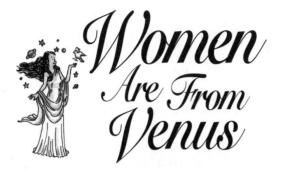

Women Are From Venus

MEN ARE FROM HELL

by Amanda Newman

Adams Media Corporation
Holbrook, Massachusetts

Published by

Adams Media Corporation
260 Center Street, Holbrook, MA 02343

ISBN: 1-58062-124-4

Printed in Canada.

J I H G F E D C B A

Library of Congress Cataloging-in-Publication Data
Newman, Amanda
Women are from Venus, men are from hell / Amanda Newman.
p.   cm.
Includes index.
ISBN 1-58062-124-4
1. Women—Quotations. 2. Men—Quotations. 3. Man-woman
relationships—Quotations, maxims, etc. 4. Men—Humor.
5. Women—Humor. 6. Man-woman relationships—Humor.
I. Title.
PN6084.W6N49   1999
082—dc21   98-45888
CIP

Cover design by Barry Littmann

This book is available at quantity discounts for bulk purchases.
For information, call 1-800-872-5627
(in Massachusetts, 781-767-8100).

Visit our home page at http://www.adamsmedia.com
Visit Amanda Newman at www.menarefromhell.com

I'd like to thank Christine, Mom and Dad, Craige and Bruce, the readers and editors who helped me pick the best stuff, and to women everywhere who love men in spite of what jerks they can be.

Contents

There Must Be Some Misunderstanding

If you can't live without me, why aren't you dead yet?

—*Cynthia Heimel (book title)*

~

Women have considerable moral sense when they don't love a man. Mighty little when they do. With men, it's the opposite. If he doesn't care for a girl, he's without scruples. If he does care, he is likely to develop a moral code only the angels can live up to.

—*Mark Reed*

They say women talk too much.
If you have worked in Congress
you know that the filibuster was
invented by men.

—*Clare Boothe Luce*

~

The most sympathetic of men
never fully comprehend woman's
concrete situation.

—*Simone de Beauvoir,*
The Second Sex *(1949)*

Why are women . . . so much more interesting to men than men are to women?

—*Virginia Woolf,*
A Room of One's Own

~

When women are depressed, they eat or go shopping. Men invade another country. It's a whole different way of thinking.

—*Elayne Boosler*

If men liked shopping, they'd call it research.

—*Cynthia Nelms*

~

A "woman driver" is one who drives like a man and gets blamed for it.

—*Patricia Ledger,*
New York Tribune *(1958)*

Ever since Eve gave Adam the apple, there has been a misunderstanding between the sexes about gifts.

—*Nan Robertson,*
New York Times *(1957)*

~

Women are not forgiven for aging. Robert Redford's lines of distinction are my old-age wrinkles.

—*Jane Fonda*

Behind every great man there is
a surprised woman.

—*Maryon Pearson*

~

If a man speaks in the forest and
there is no woman to hear him, is
he still wrong?

—*George Carlin*

~

There aren't any hard women,
just soft men.

—*Raquel Welch*

To really know a man, observe his behavior with a woman, a flat tire, and a child.

—*Anonymous*

~

Like many other women, I could not understand why every man who changed a diaper has felt impelled, in recent years, to write a book about it.

—*Barbara Ehrenreich,*
New York Times

When a woman is very, very bad, she is awful, but when a man is correspondingly good, he is weird.

—*Minna Antrim,* Naked Truths and Veiled Allusions *(1901)*

~

Men and women, women and men. It will never work.

—*Erica Jong,* Fear of Flying, *(1973)*

Men and children . . . think that
if you're sitting down it means
you're waiting for someone to
give you something to do.

—*Serena Gray,*
"Beached on the Shores of Love"

~

Why dogs are better than men:
Dogs do not play games with
you—except fetch (and they
never laugh at how you throw).

—*Anonymous*

I got divorced recently. It was a mixed marriage. I'm human, he was Klingon.

— Carol Leifer

~

He may be fat, stupid, and old, but none the less he can condemn the woman's flabby body and menopause and encounter only sympathy if he exchanges her for a younger one.

— Liv Ullmann

From my experience of life I believe my personal motto should be "Beware of men bearing flowers."

—*Muriel Spark,*
Curriculum Vitae *(1992)*

~

The real trouble about women is that they must always go on trying to adapt themselves to men's theories of women.

—*D.H. Lawrence, in*
Fear of Flying

He said he'd call me the next day, but in boy time that meant Thursday.

—*Amy Heckerling*, Clueless

~

Man to woman: "I'm not ignoring you—you've got my full peripheral attention."

—*Stephanie Piro*, Fair Game

Announcing: SEMINARS FOR
MEN COURSE 005: We Do
Not Want Sleazy Underthings
For Christmas

—Anonymous

~

What men really mean: "Of
course I like it, honey, you look
beautiful." Really means . . . "Oh,
man, what have you done to
yourself?"

—Anonymous

Face it: love isn't like it is in the movies. Walt Disney and Doris Day lied to us. I want my money back.

—*Jann Mitchell,*
Codependent For Sure

~

The main reason guys will never admit to having even the teensiest clue about what women really want is because if they did, they'd have to *do something about it*.

—*Barbara Graham*

A woman can walk through the Louvre Museum in Paris and see 5,000 breathtaking paintings on the wall. A man can walk through the Louvre Museum in Paris and see 5,000 nails in the wall. That is the inherent difference.

—*Erma Bombeck*

~

Few men are happy saying, "I don't know." They prefer, "That's not what's important here."

—*Anonymous*

I don't think the woman has been born to whom it would occur to substitute sports equipment lined up next to the wall for furniture groupings and area rugs. And yet I have frequently visited the "home" of a man who thought this was a fine idea.

—*Merrill Markoe,* What The Dogs Have Taught Me *(1992)*

~

If high heels were so wonderful, men would be wearing them.

—*Sue Grafton*

Sometimes I wonder if men and women really suit each other. Perhaps they should just live next door and just visit now and then.

—*Katharine Hepburn*

~

Women will sometimes admit making a mistake. The last man who admitted that he was wrong was General George Custer.

—*Matt Groening*

INDIFFERENCE: a woman's feeling toward a man, which is interpreted by the man as "playing hard to get."

—Anonymous

~

Most women are introspective: "Am I in love? Am I emotionally and creatively fulfilled?" Most men are outrospective: "Did my team win? How's my car?"

—Rita Rudner

For some reason, it is universally regarded as fascist to say "So?" to a woman who has just told you how she feels.

—*Roy Blount, Jr.*

~

If you believe everything between women and men is hunky-dory, then you probably don't need this book. Also, you should return to your own planet because you've grown dangerously light-headed.

— *"Jake,"* Glamour

Women: Smarter Because They Have To Be

Don't accept rides from strange
men, and remember that all men
are as strange as hell.

—*Robin Morgan,*
Sisterhood Is Powerful *(1970)*

~

The average girl would rather
have beauty than brains because
she knows that the average man
can see much better than he
can think.

—Ladies Home Journal *(1947)*

Every man who is high up loves to think that he has done it all himself; and the wife smiles, and lets it go at that. It's our only joke. Every woman knows that.

—*Sir J.M. Barrie*,
What Every Woman Knows

~

If the right man does not come along, there are many fates far worse. One is to have the wrong man come along.

—*Letitia Baldrige*,
Of Diamonds and Diplomats *(1968)*

A woman has got to love a bad man once or twice in her life, to be thankful for a good one.

—*Marjorie Kinnan Rawlings,*
The Yearling *(1938)*

~

The old theory was: "Marry an older man because they're more mature." But the new theory is: "Men don't mature. Marry a younger one."

—*Rita Rudner*

Personally, I think if a woman hasn't met the right man by the time she's 24, she may be lucky.

—Deborah Kerr

~

As long as you know that most men are like children, you know everything.

—Coco Chanel

~

Men have sight; women have insight.

—Victor Hugo

Getting along with men isn't what's truly important. The vital knowledge is how to get along with one man.

—*Phyllis McGinley*

~

God gave women intuition and femininity. Used properly, the combination easily jumbles the brain of any man I've ever met.

—*Farrah Fawcett*

A man on a date wonders if he'll get lucky. The woman already knows.

—*Monica Piper*

~

Even the wisest men make fools of themselves about women, and even the most foolish women are wise about men.

—*Dr. Theodore Reik,*
The Need To Be Loved *(1963)*

The only time a woman can
really succeed in changing a man
is when he is a baby.

—*Natalie Wood*

~

I married beneath me;
all women do.

—*Nancy Astor, in*
Dictionary of National Biography
1961–1970 (1981), p. 43

Any smart woman will tell you
that the best way to a man's heart
is through his ego.

—*Anonymous*

~

Men were only made into "men"
with great difficulty even in
primitive society. The male is not
naturally "a man" any more than
the woman. He has to be
propped up into that position
with some ingenuity, and is
always likely to collapse.

—*Wyndham Lewis*

Going to a male gynecologist is like going to a mechanic who doesn't own his own car.

—*Carrie Snow*

~

A wise woman puts a grain of sugar into everything she says to a man, and takes a grain of salt with everything he says to her.

—*Helen Rowland*

What passes for woman's intuition is often nothing more than man's transparency.

—*George Jean Nathan*

~

First time you buy a house you see how pretty the paint is and you buy it. The second time you look to see if the basement has termites. It's the same with men.

—*Lupe Velez*

Dancing is wonderful training
for girls; it's the first way you
learn to guess what a man is
going to do before he does it.

— *Christopher Morley*

~

If a man is vain, flatter. If timid,
flatter. If boastful, flatter. In all
history, too much flattery never
lost a gentleman.

— *Kathryn Cravens*,
Pursuit of Gentleman

All discarded lovers should be given a second chance, but with somebody else.

—*Mae West*

~

How can you tell the difference between men's real gifts and their guilt gifts? Guilt gifts are nicer.

—*Anonymous*

Us country women make good
wives. No matter what happens,
we've seen worse.

—*Keith Jennison*

~

Every mother knows that her
most spoiled child is her
husband.

—*Walter Winchell*

A woman doesn't care what a man looks like. They'd rather a man wouldn't be handsome, so he'll think about them instead of about himself.

—*David Graham Phillips*

~

Some women know that if they want a man made right, they'd better make him themselves.

—*Denis Boyles*, A Man's Life

All men are jackals, but you need one to protect you from the rest of them.

—*Marlene Dietrich*

~

You see a lot of smart guys with dumb women, but you hardly ever see a smart woman with a dumb guy.

—*Erica Jong*

It's a man's world, but women
are running it, secretly.

—*Cheri Oteri*

~

A man cannot ditch a woman,
because she feels it—she knows
it's coming.

—*Sinbad*

~

The only man a girl can depend
on is her daddy.

—Grease

Searching for a boy in high school is like searching for meaning in a Pauly Shore movie.

—*Amy Heckerling,* Clueless

~

A girl can wait for the right man to come along but in the meantime that still doesn't mean she can't have a wonderful time with all the wrong ones.

—*Cher*

Men:
Simple or Just
Dense?

Men are stupid and women are crazy. And the reason women are so crazy is because men are so . . . stupid.

—*George Carlin*

~

I'm not denyin' the women are foolish: God Almighty made 'em to match the men.

—*George Eliot,*
Adam Bede *(1859)*

What's with you men? Would hair stop growing on your chest if you asked directions somewhere?

—*Erma Bombeck,* When You Look Like Your Passport Photo, It's Time To Go Home

~

The man who thinks he has no faults has at least one.

—*Anonymous*

There are two periods in a man's life when he doesn't understand a woman. Before marriage and after marriage.

—*Anonymous*

~

I told someone I was getting married, and they said, "Have you picked a date yet?" I said, "Wow you can bring a date to your own wedding?" What a country!

—*Yakov Smirnoff*

What men really mean: "I'm going fishing." Really means . . . "I'm going to drink myself dangerously stupid, and stand by a stream with a stick in my hand, while the fish swim by in complete safety."

—*Anonymous*

~

If it weren't for women, men would still be wearing last week's socks.

—*Cynthia Nelms*

Why dogs are better than men:
Dogs are happy with any video
you choose to rent, because they
know the most important thing is
that you're together.

—*Anonymous*

~

Blessed is the man who, having
nothing to say, abstains from
giving us worthy evidence of
the fact.

—*George Eliot*

If men can run the world, why can't they stop wearing neckties? How intelligent is it to start the day by tying a little noose around your neck?

—*Linda Ellerbee*

~

A man who correctly guesses a woman's age may be smart, but he's not very bright.

—*Anonymous*

Men are very confident people. My husband is so confident that when he watches sports on television, he thinks that if he concentrates he can help his team. If the team is in trouble, he coaches the players from our living room, and if they're really in trouble, I have to get off the phone in case they call him.

—*Rita Rudner*

Women make fools of some
men. Other men are the do-it-
yourself type.

—Anonymous

~

There are three things most men
love but never understand:
females, girls, and women.

—Anonymous

Next to the striking of fire and the discovery of the wheel, the greatest triumph of what we call civilization was the domestication of the human male.

—*Max Lerner,*
The Unfinished Country

~

I love the male body, it's better designed than the male mind.

—*Andrea Newman,* Today
(Sept. 1988)

These are some sure-fire ways to tell if your date is too young for you. Can he fly for half fare? Are his love letters written to you in Crayola? Is his bedroom wallpapered in a clown motif? Do his pajamas have feet? When you ask him a question, does he raise his hand before answering?

—Phyllis Diller

~

A woman's guess is much more accurate than a man's certainty.

—Rudyard Kipling

Most men are boys. Men who are men are probably best, but almost impossible to find.

—*Cynthia Heimel,* If You Can't Live Without Me, Why Aren't You Dead Yet?

~

Answering "Who was that on the phone?" with "Nobody" is never going to end that conversation. Ditto for "Whose lipstick is this?"

—*Anonymous*

This bugs me the worst. That's when the husband thinks that the wife knows where everything is, huh? Like they think the uterus is a tracking device. He comes in: "Hey, Roseanne! Roseanne! Do we have any Cheetos left?" Like he can't go over and lift up that sofa cushion himself.

—*Roseanne*

~

I hate women because they always know where things are.

—*James Thurber*

There's nothing so stubborn as a man when you want him to do something.

—*Jean Giraudoux,*
The Madwoman of Chaillot

~

A man usually falls in love with the woman who asks the kind of questions he is able to answer.

—*Ronald Colman*

A man admires the woman who makes him think but he keeps away from her. He likes the woman who makes him laugh. He loves the girl who hurts him. But he marries the woman who flatters him.

—*Nellie B. Stull*

~

Women over thirty are at their best, but men over thirty are too old to recognize it.

—*Jean-Paul Belmondo*

Man: If you were a guy, you'd understand. Woman: Well, if you had ovaries, you wouldn't be so stupid!

—Suddenly Susan

~

It's relaxing to go out with my ex-wife because she already knows I'm an idiot.

—*Thomas Warren, in*
The Quotable Quote Book

Supermarkets are like giant
booby traps for males—which is
why if you send a man out to buy
eggs, sugar, and bread you
should not be surprised if he
returns home with a case of
wine, a pair of jeans, and a tree.

—*Anonymous*

~

What is the only time a man
thinks about a candlelight dinner?
When the power goes off.

—*Anonymous*

Next to activities that involve balls of many shapes and sizes, guys love to talk about how they're completely baffled by women.

—*Barbara Graham*

~

Behind every successful woman are several confused men who give her something to make fun of.

—*Sarah Miller*

Could any man ever learn that mystical thing called woman's intuition, which isn't mystical at all but rather an ability to pick up and process subtle clues that men lack because we're kind of dense?

—*Bill Cosby*, Love & Marriage

~

It is impossible to defeat an ignorant man in an argument.

—*William G. McAdoo*

What is the proper answer when the little woman asks the following question? "Can you tell I've lost weight?" A. Not really. I'd say you'd have to lose another ten pounds before it begins to show. B. If you say so. C. WOW!

—*Jean Kerr*

~

What is the thinnest book in the world? What Men Know About Women.

—*Anonymous*

A woman knows all about her children. She knows about dentist appointments and soccer games and romances and best friends and favorite foods and secret fears and hopes and dreams. A man is vaguely aware of some short people living in the house.

—Matt Groening

~

Announcing: SEMINARS FOR MEN COURSE 013: Reasons To Give Flowers

—Anonymous

A man will wear every article of clothing he owns, including his surgical pants that were hip about eight years ago, before he will do his laundry. When he is finally out of clothes, he will wear a dirty sweatshirt inside out, rent a U-Haul and take his mountain of clothes to the laundromat, and expect to meet a beautiful woman while he is there.

—*Anonymous*

Most men don't do laundry
because washers don't come with
remote controls.

—TV ad

~

I was on a date recently, and the
guy took me horseback riding.
That was kind of fun, until we
ran out of quarters.

—Susie Loucks

'Til Death . . .

There is so little difference
between husbands you may as
well keep the first.

—*Adela Rogers St. Johns*

~

Never trust a husband too far
nor a bachelor too near.

—*Helen Rowland*

Marriage is an attempt to change
a night owl into a homing pigeon.

—*Anonymous*

~

It isn't tying himself to one woman
that a man dreads when he thinks
of marrying; it's separating himself
from all the others.

—*Helen Rowland*

Being married was like having a
hippopotamus sitting on my face,
Mrs. Brown. No matter how
hard I pushed or which way I
turned, I couldn't get up. I
couldn't even breathe . . .
Hippopotamuses aren't all bad.
They are what they are. But I
wasn't meant to have one sitting
on my face.

—*Faith Sullivan,*
The Cape Ann *(1988)*

You know that the urge for revenge is a fact of marital life.

—*Jane Smiley,* Good Will *(1989)*

~

The only thing that keeps me from being happily married . . . is my husband.

—*Andra Douglas*

~

I used to live alone . . . then I got a divorce.

—*Greeting card*

Any woman who still thinks
marriage is a 50-50 proposition
is only proving that she doesn't
understand either men or
percentages.

—*Florynce Kennedy*

~

Mrs. Smith said that she could
always tell when her husband
was lying. If his lips were
moving, he was.

—*Anonymous*

Man of few words: one who
takes three hours to tell you he is
a man of few words; husband.

—Anonymous

~

The man who boasts he never
made a mistake is often married
to a woman who did.

—Anonymous

My husband said he needed more space, so I locked him outside.

—*Roseanne*

~

I'd marry again if I found a man who had fifteen million dollars, would sign over half to me, and guarantee that he'd be dead within a year.

—*Bette Davis*

If brides, they should be very cautious about asking their husbands to dry the dinner dishes. The right start is important to a marriage. Make them wash 'em right from the beginning.

—*Georgie Starbuck Galbraith, "Horoscope for Housewives," McCall's (1963)*

~

An archeologist is the best husband any woman can have: the older she gets, the more interested he is in her.

—*Agatha Christie (1954)*

I'll tell you the real secret of how to stay married. Keep the cave clean. Sharpen his spear, and stick it in his hand when he goes out in the morning to spear that bear; and when the bear chases him, console him when he comes home at night, and tell him what a big man he is, and then hide the spear so he doesn't fall over it and stab himself . . .

—*Jerome Chodorov and Joseph Fields*, Anniversary Waltz

Only one woman in ten recognizes her husband as the same man he was before she married him. Nine out of ten say he's changed. One in three says he's changed for the worse.

—*Gallup Survey, "The Woman's Mind,"* Ladies' Home Journal *(1962)*

~

Husbands are like fires. They go out when unattended.

—*Zsa Zsa Gabor,* Newsweek *(1960)*

Fat generally tends to make a man a better husband. His wife is happy in the knowledge she is not married to a woman chaser. Few fat men chase girls, because they get winded too easily.

—*Hal Boyle*

~

All husbands are alike, but they have different faces so you can tell them apart.

—*Anonymous*

If love means never having to say you're sorry, then marriage means always having to say everything twice.

—*Estelle Getty*

~

I've been married to one Marxist and one Fascist, and neither one would take the garbage out.

—*Lee Grant*

Announcing: SEMINARS FOR MEN COURSE 002: You Too Can Do Housework

—Anonymous

~

Marrying a man is like buying something you've been admiring for a long time in a shop window. You may love it when you get it home, but it doesn't always go with everything else in the house.

—Jean Kerr

A California woman says her husband is at the dangerous age when all females look alike to him—desirable!

—*Anonymous*

~

The man who owes it all to his wife seldom pays her back.

—*Anonymous*

~

Eat, drink, and re-marry.

—*Post-it notes*

Get a job, your husband hates you. Get a good job, your husband leaves you. Get a stupendous job, your husband leaves you for a teenager.

—*Cynthia Heimel*

~

If a woman laughs at her husband's joke, it means he has told a new joke or he has a new wife.

—*Anonymous*

You can always surprise your husband on your anniversary just by mentioning it.

—*Al Schlock*

~

If we did get a divorce, the only way he would know it is if they would announce it on *Wide World of Sports*.

—*Dr. Joyce Brothers*
on her sports addict husband

Divorce? No. Murder? Yes.

> —Anne Hayes, wife of Ohio State
> football coach Woody Hayes, when asked
> whether she had ever considered divorce

~

Marriage isn't a 50-50 proposition
very often. It's more like 100-0
one moment and 0-100 the next.

> —Billie Jean King

What men really mean: "'Uh huh,' 'Sure, honey,' or 'Yes, dear.'" Really means . . . absolutely nothing. It's a conditioned response like Pavlov's dog drooling.

—*Anonymous*

~

Husband: How come you never tell me when you enjoy sex? Wife: Because you're never home.

—*Joey Adams*

I had only one friend, my dog. My wife was mad at me, and I told her a man ought to have at least two friends. She agreed—and bought me another dog.

—*Pepper Rodgers,*
college football coach

~

When men reach their sixties and retire, they go to pieces. Women go right on cooking.

—*Gail Sheehy*

American husbands are the best in the world; no other husbands are so generous to their wives, or can be so easily divorced.

—*Elinor Glyn*

~

Pretend to treat your wife as a rational creature. It may surprise her at first, but she'll appreciate it. On the other hand, she may burst out crying—thinking you're drunk again.

—*Anonymous*

Marriage originates when a man meets the only woman who really understands him. So does divorce.

—Ohio State Sun Dial

~

All a man expects his wife to be is a sweetheart, a valet, an audience, and a nurse.

—*Anonymous*

Marriage entitles women to the protection of strong men who steady the stepladder for them while they paint the kitchen ceiling.

—Anonymous

~

Try praising your wife, even it it does frighten her at first.

—Billy Sunday

There are no records to prove it, mind you, but I have every reason to believe my husband was an eleventh month baby. And he's been running two months late ever since.

—*Erma Bombeck*

~

When a party reveler asks, "Have you ever thought of leaving your husband" and you answer, "Where?" you're married.

—*Erma Bombeck*

I know what I wish Ralph Nader
would investigate next.
Marriage. It's not safe, it's not
safe at all.

—*Jean Kerr,* Penny Candy

~

"Left Hand" is the hand that
every married man in a singles
bar keeps in his pocket.

—*Nancy Linn-Desmond*

Men hate to lose. I once beat my husband at tennis. I asked him, "Are we going to have sex again?" He said, "Yes, but not with each other."

—*Rita Rudner*

~

Trust your husband, adore your husband, and get as much as you can in your own name.

—*Joan Rivers*

This Is Equality?

Whatever women do they must do twice as well as men to be thought half as good. Luckily, this is not difficult.

—*Charlotte Whitton,*
Mayor of Ottawa (1963)

~

Ginger Rogers did everything that Fred Astaire did. She just did it backwards and in high heels.

—*Variously attributed to*
Faith Whittlesey, Linda Ellerbee,
and Ann Richards

Like every good little feminist-in-training in the sixties, I burned my bra—and now it's the nineties and I realize Playtex had supported me better than any man I've ever known . . .

—*Susan Sweetzer*

~

When a woman demands equal rights, she is simply indulging in flattery.

—*Anonymous*

I have yet to hear a man ask for advice on how to combine marriage and a career.

—*Gloria Steinem*

~

I'm furious about the Women's Liberationists. They keep getting up on soapboxes and proclaiming that women are brighter than men. That's true, but it should be kept quiet or it ruins the whole racket.

—*Anita Loos*

If you want something said, ask a man; if you want something done, ask a woman.

—*Margaret Thatcher*

~

Women who seek to be equal with men lack ambition.

—*Timothy Leary*

~

A woman without a man is like a fish without a bicycle.

—*Gloria Steinem*

Whether women are better than men I cannot say—but I can say they are certainly no worse.

—*Golda Meir*

~

If men could get pregnant, abortion would be a sacrament.

—*Florynce Kennedy*

Some men think they have an inferiority complex, when, in fact, they are just inferior.

—*Anonymous*

~

I don't mind living in a man's world as long as I can be a woman in it.

—*Marilyn Monroe*

There is very little difference between men and women in space.

—*Helen Sharman, British astronaut*

~

A man can sleep around, no questions asked, but if a woman makes nineteen or twenty mistakes she's a tramp.

—*Joan Rivers*

How do some men define Roe vs. Wade? Two ways to cross a river.

—*Anonymous*

~

Don't kid yourself: telling a woman that you stopped by the local pub on your way home, but neglecting to mention that you spent the entire time with a teen model named Daphne in the back of her Jeep Cherokee is the same as telling a lie.

—*Barbara Graham,*
Women Who Run With the Poodles

This book is dedicated to Queen Isabella of Spain. Without her, the New World, and hence the Pittsburgh Steelers, the Hoover Dam, and Ernest Hemingway, would not have been possible — and Christopher Columbus would have ended up sipping sangria and eating quiche in Lisbon. Naturally, he took all the credit.

—*Joyce Jillson*,
Real Women Don't Pump Gas

Lowlifes

Eighty percent of married men cheat in America. The rest cheat in Europe.

—*Jackie Mason*

~

Paula Jones is suing President Clinton for $700,000 for allegedly proposing she perform a sex act on him. In that case, every woman in America is owed millions by construction workers.

—*Elayne Boosler*

He was the most self-involved guy I ever met in my life. He had a coffee mug on his table that said, "I'm the greatest." He had a plaque on the wall that said, "I'm number one." And on his bedspread it said, "The Best." In the middle of making love he said, "Move over—you're getting in my way."

—*Karen Haber*

"I am not just another notch on your belt?" she asked him. "Of course not," he said as he put a mark on the chalkboard.

—*Jay Leno*

~

Outside every thin woman is a fat man trying to get in.

—*Katherine Whitehorn*

Whenever you want to marry someone, go have lunch with his ex-wife.

—*Shelley Winters*

~

A bachelor is a guy who leans toward women, but not far enough to lose his balance.

—*Anonymous*

Classic male excuse hall of fame: "Don't take it personally." "I do love you as a friend." "But you never asked me if I was married with kids!" "Our break-up has nothing to do with ____. (Put her name here.) "I just need some space." "(I lied because) I didn't want to hurt your feelings." "It's not what you think . . . " "I thought *you* were using birth control."

—*Anonymous*

When this judge let a rapist go because the woman had been wearing a miniskirt and so was "asking for it" I thought, "Ladies, what we all should do is this: next time we see an ugly guy on the street, shoot him. After all, he knew he was ugly when he left the house. He was asking for it."

—*Ellen Cleghorn*

~

We had a lot in common; I loved him and he loved him.

—*Shelley Winters*

In passing, also, I would like to say that the first time Adam had a chance he laid the blame on woman . . .

—*Nancy Astor,*
My Two Countries

~

When a man tells me he's going to put all his cards on the table, I always look up his sleeve.

—*Leslie Hore-Belisha*

I wasn't kissing her. I was whispering in her mouth.

—*Chico Marx, when his wife caught him kissing a chorus girl*

~

Women dream of world peace, a safe environment, and eliminating hunger. What do men dream of? Being stuck in an elevator with the Doublemint twins.

—*Anonymous*

I had to hold down three jobs to put him through school. Then when I turned 26 and thought I should go back to college, he divorced me. For a 19-year-old bimbette with straw for brains who walks seven feet behind him so that when he stops to read a road map she wipes his butt. But I'm not bitter.

—*Diane Ford*

He was like a cock who
thought the sun had risen to
hear him crow.

—George Eliot

~

I just want him to call so I
can tell him I never want to see
him again.

—Bill Cosby

~

Why dogs are better than men:
Dogs mean it when they kiss you.

—Anonymous

The next morning, Crash was gone. It's not like it was the first time I'd gone to bed with a man and woke up with a note.

—*Ron Shelton,* Bull Durham

~

When a man is wrapped up in himself, he makes a pretty small package.

—*Ruskin*

Total Slams

Q: What's the difference between men and pigs? A: Pigs don't get drunk and act like men.

—*Anonymous*

~

There are no great men, buster. There are only men.

—*Charles Schnee,*
The Bad and The Beautiful

Ninety-nine percent of men
give the other one percent a
bad name.

—*Anonymous*

~

If they can put one man on the
moon why can't they put them
all there?

—*Chocolate Waters*

Have you ever wondered why men who haven't had a date in six months know what women really want?

—*Anonymous*

~

A man's home may seem to be his castle on the outside; inside it is more often his nursery.

—*Clare Boothe Luce*

You never see a man walking down the street with a woman who has a pot belly and a bald spot.

—*Elayne Boosler*

~

Can you imagine a world without men? No crime and lots of happy fat women.

—*Nicole Hollander*

If a man watches three football games in a row, he should be declared legally dead.

—*Erma Bombeck*

~

Announcing: SEMINARS FOR MEN COURSE 020: You Too Can Be A Designated Driver

—*Anonymous*

Men! The only animal in the world to fear!

—*D.H. Lawrence*

~

Statistics show there are three ages when men misbehave: young, old, and middle.

—*Anonymous*

History records only one
indispensable man: Adam.

—*Anonymous*

~

Why dogs are better than men:
You can train a dog.

—*Anonymous*

~

Some men grow; others just swell.

—*Anonymous*

When a male heckler called out, "Are you a lesbian?" she immediately replied, "Are you my alternative?"

—*Florynce Kennedy*

~

Not all guys are icky . . . I mean, look at Tom Cruise . . . but most of them are disgusting.

—*Anonymous*

What are two reasons why men don't mind their own business? No mind, no business.

—Anonymous

~

Have you ever wondered why men who aren't on speaking terms with their families know how to achieve peace in the Middle East?

—Anonymous

There are many words you could use to describe men today. You could say they are charming, strong, caring. . . . You would be wrong, but you could say them.

—*Anonymous*

~

Conceit is God's gift to little men.

—*Bruce Barton*

Talk to a man about himself and he will listen for hours.

—*Disraeli*

~

I want a perfume that says to a man, "Go to Hell!"

—*C. Sele, cartoon*

~

The only problem with women is men.

—*Kathie Sarachild*

Guys On Guys

To get a man's attention, just stand in front of the TV and don't move. He'll talk to you. I promise.

— *Tim Allen*

~

The most difficult secret for a man to keep is his own opinion of himself.

—*Marcel Pagnol*

Shame is the feeling you have
when you agree with the woman
who loves you that you are the
man she thinks you are.

—*Carl Sandburg*

~

In love, women are professionals,
men are amateurs.

—*Francois Truffaut*

Men, in general, are but great
children.

—*Napoleon*

~

I think it can be stated without
denial that no man ever saw a
man he would be willing to
marry if he were a woman.

—*George Gibbs,*
How To Stay Married

The wedding is a beautiful thing.
I think the idea behind the tuxedo
is the woman's point of view that
"Men are all the same, we might
as well dress them that way."

—*Jerry Seinfeld*

~

The same time that women
came up with PMS, men came
up with ESPN.

—*Blake Clark*

Sigmund Freud once said, "What do women want?" The only thing I have learned in fifty-two years is that women want men to stop asking dumb questions like that.

—*Bill Cosby*

~

Being a woman is a terribly difficult task since it consists principally in dealing with men.

—*Joseph Conrad*

An American Monkey after
getting drunk on Brandy would
never touch it again, and thus is
much wiser than most men.

—*Charles Darwin*

~

There are two things no man will
admit he cannot do well: drive
and make love.

—*Stirling Moss*

When a young man complains
that a young lady has no heart, it
is a pretty certain sign that she
has his.

—*George D. Prentice*

~

Any man who says he doesn't
desire to have sex with a woman
he thinks is attractive is lying.

—*Corbin Bernsen*

Men build bridges and throw railroads across deserts, and yet they contend successfully that the job of sewing on a button is beyond them. Accordingly, they don't have to sew buttons.

—*Heywood Broun (1921)*

~

Men get to be a mixture of the charming mannerisms of the women they have known.

—*F. Scott Fitzgerald,*
The Crack-Up *(1945)*

Most men do not mature, they simply grow taller.

—*Leo Rosten*

~

No man ever told a woman she talked too much when she was telling him how wonderful he is.

—*Earl Wilson*

Some women . . . enjoy tremendously being told they look a mess—and they actually thrill to the threat of physical violence. I've never met one that does, mind you, but they probably do exist. In books. By men.

> —*Alan Ayckbourn*, Round and Round the Garden *(1975)*

Men never learn anything about women, but they have a lot of fun trying.

—*Olin Miller*

~

A man may be so totally lost to hope that he will refuse to believe he can ever do or be anything, but few ever get so far down that they can't imagine a woman might be in love with them.

—*H.L. Davis*

Guys start acting macho at an early age. Any parent will tell you that girl babies will generally display a wide-eyed curiosity about the world, whereas boy babies will generally try to destroy it.

—*Dave Barry*

Man today obviously needs work. Some need a kinder, more caring outlook. Some need a heightened appreciation of woman, his fellow creature on the planet whom he has been neglecting lately. Some men you just want to run up to and slap. Others have bad posture and poor eating habits. Man needs major work, and I'm afraid it's going to be expensive.

—*Frank Gannon,*
All About Man

The rooster makes more racket
than the hen that lays the egg.

—*Joel Chandler Harris*

~

Whenever you see a man with
handkerchief, socks, and tie to
match, you may be sure he is
wearing a present.

—*Frank Case*

The majority of husbands remind me of an orangutan trying to play the violin.

—*Balzac*

~

You know why men lie to women so much? Because women don't believe them anyway!

—*Roy Blount, Jr.*

Men just don't say anything
meaningful to each other unless
they're really drunk. Sometimes
while jogging together. It's
tradition.

—*Peter Nelson*

~

There's only three types of men
in the world: the loving, the
faithful, and the majority.

—*Richard Jeni*

Most men act so tough and strong on the outside because on the inside, we are scared, weak, and fragile. Men, not women, are the weaker sex.

—*Jerry Rubin,* Chicago Tribune
(March, 1978)

The Secret Lives of Men

What men really mean: "It's a guy thing." Really means . . . "There is no rational thought pattern connected with it, and you have no chance at all of making it logical."

—*Anonymous*

~

Every man has a secret ambition to outsmart horses, fish, and women.

—*Anonymous*

Women have one great advantage over men. It is commonly thought that if they marry they have done enough, and need career no further. If a man marries, on the other hand, public opinion is all against him if he takes this view.

—*Rose Macaulay,*
A Casual Commentary *(1926)*

Remember when I told you that
I didn't love you no more? Well
I lied.

—*Robert Cray, "Well I Lied"*

~

How many roads must a man
travel down before he admits
he's lost?

—*Anonymous*

Men can read maps better than women. 'Cause only the male mind could conceive of one inch equaling a hundred miles.

—*Roseanne*

~

I sleep with my teddy bear because I know where he's been.

—*Anonymous*

The man who has no secrets
from his wife either has no
secrets or no wife.

—*Anonymous*

~

The trouble with marriage is
that, while every woman is at
heart a mother, every man is at
heart a bachelor.

—*E.V. Lucas*

Boys will be boys, and so will a lot of middle-aged men.

—*Kin Hubbard*

~

Men invented language to satisfy their deep need to complain.

—*Lily Tomlin*

Men 30 to 39 years old think about sex every 15 minutes. After 40, the frequency drops to once every half hour.

—Men's Health Magazine *(1990)*

~

Most accidents occur in the home. Many men use this as an excuse to stay out late.

—*Anonymous*

Few women admit their age. Few men act theirs.

—*Anonymous*

~

Why dogs are better than men: Gorgeous dogs don't know they're gorgeous.

—*Anonymous*

Teen-age boys who whistle at girls are just going through a stage which will probably last fifty years.

—Anonymous

~

Chivalry is a man's inclination to defend a woman against every man but himself.

—Anonymous

I've been asked when lying to a woman is okay. All the time would be just fine. As long as you don't get caught. Just don't get caught.

— Tim Allen

~

The intimate revelations of young men, or at least the terms in which they express them, are usually plagiaristic and marred by obvious suppressions.

— F. Scott Fitzgerald,
The Great Gatsby *(1925)*

The tragedy of machismo is that a man is never quite man enough.

—*Germaine Greer, "My Mailer Problem," in* Esquire *(1971)*

~

A romantic man often feels more uplifted with two women than with one: his love seems to hit the ideal mark somewhere between two different faces.

—*Elizabeth Bowen,*
The Death of the Heart

Upscale young men seem to go for the kind of woman who plays with a full deck of credit cards, who won't cry when she's knocked to the ground while trying to board the six o'clock Eastern shuttle, and whose schedule doesn't allow for a sexual encounter lasting more than twelve minutes.

—Barbara Ehrenreich, "The Cult of Busyness," New York Times (1985)

Beware of men who cry. It's true that men who cry are sensitive to and in touch with their feelings, but the only feelings they tend to be sensitive to and in touch with are their own.

—*Nora Ephron,* Heartburn

~

When a man brings his wife flowers for no reason—there's a reason.

—*Molly McGee*

Never worry for fear you have broken a man's heart: at the worst it is only sprained and a week's rest will put it in perfect working order again.

—*Helen Rowland*,
Reflections of a Bachelor Girl

~

If there is anything disagreeable going on, men are always sure to get out of it. . . .

—*Jane Austen*,
Northanger Abbey

If a woman wears gay colors, rouge, and a startling hat, a man hesitates to take her out. If she wears a little turban and a tailored suit, he takes her out and stares all evening at a woman in gay colors, rouge, and a startling hat.

—Baltimore Beacon

~

Men are always ready to respect anything that bores them.

—*Marilyn Monroe*

What men really mean: "Good idea." Really means . . . "It'll never work. And I'll spend the rest of the day gloating."

—Anonymous

~

You men are unaccountable things; mad till you have your mistresses, and then stark mad till you are rid of 'em again.

—John Vanbrugh,
The Provoked Wife *(1697)*

There is nothing about which men lie so much as about their sexual powers. In this at least every man is, what in his heart he would like to be, a Casanova.

— *W. Somerset Maugham,*
A Writer's Notebook *(1949)*

~

He who believes in nothing still needs a girl to believe in him.

—*Eugen Rosenstock-Huessy*

To men, porno movies are beautiful love stories with all the boring stuff taken out.

—*Richard Jeni*

~

"Young" is an adjective used by men to describe a woman who is under 18 or a man who is under 80.

—*Nancy Linn-Desmond*

What remains a mystery about
men? Their reticence. I mean,
fling the door open and live your
freakin' life. Feel your feelings.
Be a man.

—*Ashley Judd, in* GQ *(Jan. 1997)*

~

Man to woman: "You think I
don't have any feelings! Well,
lust counts as a feeling . . .
doesn't it?"

—*Stephanie Piro*

Of course the single life has problems—having two lovers is a scheduling problem, and three is a real test of a man's organizational ability, and yet those are the very problems a man hopes for, Figaro.

—*Garrison Keillor,*
The Book of Guys

~

Men like to barbecue. Men will cook if danger is involved.

—*Rita Rudner*

Wouldn't it be great if you could just be honest with a woman you find attractive and say, "Hi. I'm Bob. You're very attractive. Want to go home and rut like weasels?"

— *Tim Allen*

~

Women love cats. Men say they love cats, but when women aren't looking, men kick cats.

—*Matt Groening*

A survey was taken on the
nocturnal habits of men. The
results showed that 5 percent of
the men get up to drink a glass of
water, 10 percent to go to the
bathroom, and 85 percent get up
to go home.

—*Joe Uris, in* Say It Again,
ed. Dorothy Uris

~

Men love to talk about politics,
but they often forget to do
political things such as voting.

—*Anonymous*

Men can't know what it's like to be pregnant, and women can't know what it's like to have an organ which is half voluntary, half involuntary. We're in a much better position to understand penises than you are, and we don't even know what's going on, sometimes.

—*Peter Nelson*

To a woman, having flowers sent
to her is thoughtful. To a man,
sending flowers is a way of being
thoughtful without putting any
thought into it. It's like foreign aid.

—*Roy Blount, Jr.*

~

Interesting: a word a man uses to
describe a woman who lets him
do all the talking.

—*Anonymous*

Announcing: SEMINARS FOR
MEN COURSE 021: Honest—
You Don't Look Like Mel
Gibson—Especially Naked

—*Anonymous*

~

Girls are always running through
my mind. They don't dare walk.

—*Andy Gibb*

The Sex Part

How can you tell if a man is sexually excited? He's breathing.

—*Anonymous*

~

Men are those creatures with two legs and eight hands.

—*Jayne Mansfield*

If men really knew how to do it,
they wouldn't have to pay for it.

—*Roseanne*

~

Dr. Ruth says we women should
tell our lovers how to make love
to us. My boyfriend goes nuts if I
tell him how to drive!

—*Pam Stone*

The male attitude toward sex is like squirting jam into a doughnut.

—*Germaine Greer*

~

A lot of guys think the larger a woman's breasts are, the less intelligent she is. I don't think it works like that. I think it's the opposite. I think the larger a woman's breasts are, the less intelligent the men become.

—*Anita Wise*

An Irishman is the only man in the world who will step over the bodies of a dozen naked women to get to a bottle of stout.

—*Unknown*

~

A man's sexuality goes through three stages: tri-weekly, try-weekly, and try-weakly.

—*Sydnie Meltzer Kleinhenz*

Snuggle: an act of warmth that your husband will inevitably interpret as foreplay.

— *Tom Carey*

~

Why dogs are better than men: Dogs understand what "no" means.

— *Anonymous*

Condoms should be marketed in 3 sizes, jumbo, colossal, and super colossal, so that men do not have to go in and ask for the small.

—*Barbara Seaman*

~

By keeping men off, you keep them on.

—*Gay (1688–1732)*

He doesn't want to take a girl out and do things—he'd rather take her in and undo things.

—Anonymous

~

What men really mean: "I was listening to you. It's just that I have things on my mind." Really means . . . "I was wondering if that red-head over there is wearing a bra."

—Anonymous

Women complain about sex more than men. Their gripes fall into two major categories: (1) Not enough. (2) Too much.

—*Ann Landers*

~

Women prefer 30–40 minutes of foreplay. Men prefer 30–40 seconds of foreplay. Men consider driving back to her place as part of the foreplay.

—*Matt Groening*

If love is blind, why are so
many men attracted to a
beautiful woman?

—Anonymous

~

Most men have a way with
women, but it's seldom their own.

—Anonymous

"Please, I'll only put it in for a minute." She replies with, "What does he think I am, a microwave?"

—*Beverly Mickins*

~

Give a man a free hand and he'll run it all over you.

—*Mae West*

The clothes that keep a man looking his best are worn by girls on beaches.

— *Walter Woerner*

~

If half the engineering effort and public interest that go into the research on the American bosom had gone into our guided-missile program, we would now be running hot-dog stands on the moon.

— *Al Capp*

I've always resisted the notion that there is canine in every guy, and yet, that sure would explain a few things, not the least of which is this oxymoron: Pamela Anderson Lee, "actress."

—Leonard Pitts, Jr.

~

What a man enjoys about a woman's clothes are his fantasies of how she would look without them.

—Brendan Francisin, in
1,911 Best Things Anybody Ever Said

Why don't men often show their true feelings? Because they don't have any.

—*Anonymous*

~

Why do so many women fake orgasm? Because so many men fake foreplay.

—*Anonymous*

Fondle the woman in your life once for every thousand times you play with your private parts. That should be just about right.

—*Barbara Graham*

~

Woman, observing that her mate went out of his way to make himself entertaining, rightly surmised that sex had something to do with it.

—*E.B. White,*
The Sexual Revolution

He gave her a look that you could have poured on a waffle.

—*Ring Lardner*

~

Men in lust aren't interested in quality.

—*Peter Nelson*

A woman isn't just a collection of buttons for a man to press, a collection of erotic knee jerks.

—*Camille Cosby*

~

We live in far too permissive a society. Never before has pornography been this rampant. And those films are lit so badly!

—*Woody Allen*

I'm in love . . . I mean, this guy is so sweet, he even kisses me before we do it.

—*Laura Kightlinger*

~

I suspect your version of romance is whatever'll separate me from my panties.

—*Laurian Leggett,*
Doc Hollywood

Easy: a term used to describe a
woman who has the sexual
morals of a man.

—Anonymous

~

Announcing: SEMINARS FOR
MEN COURSE 014: How To
Stay Awake After Sex

—Anonymous

What's a man's idea of foreplay?
A half hour of begging.

—Anonymous

~

Men and women can never be
friends because the sex part gets
in the way.

—Nora Ephron,
When Harry Met Sally

Fear of the "C" Word

If you want to scare your boyfriend next Halloween, come dressed as what he fears most. Commitment.

—*Peter Nelson,*
Real Man Tells All

~

A woman feels a man's love should be like a toothbrush. It shouldn't be shared.

—*Anonymous*

A man's heart is like a sponge—
soaked with emotion and
sentiment. He can squeeze out a
little bit for every pretty woman
he meets.

—Anonymous

~

Apparently men rarely dream
about getting married. Well, that
figures. Women have a magazine
called *Bride*, but there's no
magazine for men called *Groom*.

—Mary Reinholz

A girl's hardest task is to prove to a man that his intentions are serious.

—Helen Rowland

~

Men do not settle down. Men surrender.

—Chris Rock

Guys are born with a fundamental, genetically transmitted mental condition known to psychologists as: The Fear That If You Get Attached to a Woman, Some Unattached Guy, Somewhere, Will Be Having More Fun Than You.

—*Dave Barry*

~

They call him the "Dry Cleaner"—he works fast and leaves no ring.

—*Anonymous*

"I can't tell you how much I love you," he said. "Try," she said. "I'm very fond of you," he said. "Nice try," she said.

—*Charles Schulz*

~

Some men think that being married to a woman means merely seeing her in the mornings instead of in the evenings.

—*Helen Rowland*

"Geographically undesirable" is a term used by a man to describe a woman who is not a good dating prospect because she is either more than a 15-minute drive away or else lives near enough to see what time he comes home and with whom.

—*Nancy Linn-Desmond*

To a woman the words "I love you" represent a heartfelt expression of the intensely fond feelings you have for her. At least, this kind of thing will be what the woman has in mind when she utters the words, and so she will not be pleased if your response is "thank you" or "I know."

—*Merrill Markoe*

A man does not call a relationship a relationship—he refers to it as "that time when me and Suzie were boinking on a semi-regular basis."

—*Matt Groening*

~

Announcing: SEMINARS FOR MEN COURSE 008: Parenting: It Doesn't End With Conception

—*Anonymous*

"I'm sorry," guys are always telling women, "but I'm just not ready to make a commitment." Guys are in a permanent state of nonreadiness. If guys were turkey breasts, you could put them in a 350-degree oven on July Fourth, and they still wouldn't be done in time for Thanksgiving.

—*Dave Barry*

Can't Live
With 'Em...

Men are the enemy, but I still love the enemy.

—*Cameron Crowe*,
Jerry McGuire

~

There are men I could spend eternity with. But not this life.

—*Kathleen Norris*,
The Middle of the World

Q: When did God create men?
A: When she realized that
vibrators couldn't dance or
buy drinks.

—Anonymous

~

The male is a domestic animal
which, if treated with firmness
and kindness, can be trained to
do most things.

—Jilly Cooper

If you haven't had at least a slight poetic crack in the heart, you have been cheated by nature. Because a broken heart is what makes life so wonderful five years later, when you see the guy in an elevator and he is fat and smoking a cigar and saying, "Long time no see."

—*Phyllis Batelle,*
New York Journal-American *(1962)*

Announcing: SEMINARS FOR
MEN COURSE 022: The
Obtainable Goal: Omitting "/@#*
From Your Vocabulary

—Anonymous

~

For though I know he loves
me/Tonight my heart is sad/His
kiss was not so wonderful/As all
the dreams I had.

—Sara Teasdale

When women go wrong, men go right after them.

—*Mae West*

~

Whenever I date a guy, I think, is this the man I want my children to spend their weekends with?

—*Rita Rudner*

Many men are slow but sure.
Others are just slow.

—*Anonymous*

~

If a man tells a woman she's
beautiful, she'll overlook most of
his other lies.

—*Anonymous*

Q: What do you do when your boyfriend walks out: A: Shut the door.

—*Angela Martin*

~

My mother's two categories: nice men did things for you, bad men did things to you.

—*Margaret Atwood*, Lady Oracle

Sure I want a man in my life,
but not in my house. I want him
to hook up the VCR and leave.
Why should I want him in the
house?

—*Joy Behar*

~

You have to kiss an awful lot of
frogs before you get a prince.

—*Graffito*

They say that men suffer/As badly, as long/I worry, I worry/In case they are wrong.

— *Wendy Cope, "I Worry" (1992)*

~

Men: can't live without 'em, can't leave 'em by the side of the road.

— *Unknown*

I like the concept of "men" . . . It's
the reality I have problems with!

—*Stephanie Piro,* Fair Game

~

Bumper sticker: Life's too short
to dance with ugly men.

—*Anonymous*

Good dates don't necessarily
make good mates.

—*Barnett Brickner, in*
A Treasury of the Art of Living

~

Though love can make the world
go round, It often makes the
world go flat.

—*Margaret Fishback,*
"I Stand Corrected"

You're not one of those women who tries to fix men, are you? Because men cannot be fixed.

—*Ron Shelton,* Tin Cup

~

It's always boys . . . that's all you want in high school. I don't care how old you get, it's still boys.

—*Sandra Bullock*

Reasons we like men just the way they are: They're enthusiastic about our bodies, even when we're not.

They're at peace with their bodies, except for maybe some minor anxiety over height, baldness, and/or penis size.

Their unapologetic lust for a nice hunk of beef or chocolate cake.

Their genuine ardor for tinkering with toilets, changing oil and assembling gas grills—jobs any intelligent woman can do but would be nuts to volunteer for.

How awestruck they are in the face of a Wonderbra or a homemade cookie.

—Anonymous

To all my boyfriends—past, present, and future: I love you. I hate you. I miss you. I want my money back. Choose the one that applies to you.

—*Kim Coles*

~

"I hate men!" she says as she goes back for more.

—*Katie Shulte*

101 Reasons Why A Cat Is Better Than A Man

By Allia Zobel, Illustrated by Nicole Hollander

Trade paperback, 80 pages
ISBN: 1-55850-436-2, $5.95

Honestly, now: Which would you rather face—life without cats or life without men?

If you had any hesitation about opting for a feline companion, you need to read *101 Reasons Why A Cat Is Better Than A Man*. It provides irreverent, occasionally imprudent, always on-target confirmation of what women have long suspected: You're better off with a cat.

101 More Reasons Why A Cat Is Better Than A Man

By Allia Zobel, Illustrated by Nicole Hollander

If you've ever had to make the choice between a cat and a man, here's proof that you're better off with kitty—cats are never late for dinner, don't get cold feet, and couldn't care less whether you've balanced your checkbook!

This irreverent collection confirms what you've always suspected—a cat is a woman's best friend!

Trade paperback, 80 pages
ISBN: 1-55850-794-9, $6.95